this book belongs to:

_____

_____

_____

Email us at

modernkidpress@gmail.com

to get free extras!

_____

Just title the email "Kids Gratitude"

And we will send some extra

surprises your way!

DATE: S M T W TH F S ___/___/___

I'M THANKFUL FOR

1. _____

2. _____

3. _____

THIS PERSON BROUGHT ME JOY TODAY:

_____

I FEEL: 🙂   🙂   😐   🙁   ☹️

WHAT WAS THE BEST PART ABOUT YOUR DAY?
DRAW OR WRITE ABOUT IT!

DATE: S M T W TH F S ___ / ___ / ___

I'M THANKFUL FOR

1. _____

2. _____

3. _____

THIS PERSON BROUGHT ME JOY TODAY:

_____

I FEEL: ☺ ☺ ☺ ☹ ☹

WHAT WAS THE BEST PART ABOUT YOUR DAY?
DRAW OR WRITE ABOUT IT!

DATE: S M T W TH F S ___ / ___ / ___

I'M THANKFUL FOR

1. _____

2. _____

3. _____

THIS PERSON BROUGHT ME JOY TODAY:

_____

I FEEL: ☺ ☺ 😐 ☹ ☹

WHAT WAS THE BEST PART ABOUT YOUR DAY?
DRAW OR WRITE ABOUT IT!

DATE: S   M   T   W   TH   F   S   ___ / ___ / ___

I'M THANKFUL FOR

1. _____

2. _____

3. _____

THIS PERSON BROUGHT ME JOY TODAY:

_____

I FEEL: ☺   🙂   😐   🙁   ☹

WHAT WAS THE BEST PART ABOUT YOUR DAY?
DRAW OR WRITE ABOUT IT!

DATE: S   M   T   W   TH   F   S   ___ / ___ / ___

I'M THANKFUL FOR

1. _____

2. _____

3. _____

THIS PERSON BROUGHT ME JOY TODAY:

_____

I FEEL: ☺   🙂   😐   🙁   ☹

WHAT WAS THE BEST PART ABOUT YOUR DAY?
DRAW OR WRITE ABOUT IT!

DATE: S M T W TH F S ___ / ___ / ___

I'M THANKFUL FOR

1. _____

2. _____

3. _____

THIS PERSON BROUGHT ME JOY TODAY:

_____

I FEEL: ☺ 🙂 😐 🙁 ☹

WHAT WAS THE BEST PART ABOUT YOUR DAY?
DRAW OR WRITE ABOUT IT!

DATE: S M T W TH F S ___ / ___ / ___

I'M THANKFUL FOR

1. _____

2. _____

3. _____

THIS PERSON BROUGHT ME JOY TODAY:

_____

I FEEL: ☺ 🙂 😐 🙁 ☹

WHAT WAS THE BEST PART ABOUT YOUR DAY?
DRAW OR WRITE ABOUT IT!

DATE: S M T W TH F S ___ / ___ / ___

I'M THANKFUL FOR

1. _____

2. _____

3. _____

THIS PERSON BROUGHT ME JOY TODAY:

_____

I FEEL: ☺ 🙂 😐 🙁 ☹

WHAT WAS THE BEST PART ABOUT YOUR DAY?
DRAW OR WRITE ABOUT IT!

DATE: S   M   T   W   TH   F   S   ___ / ___ / ___

I'M THANKFUL FOR

1. _____

2. _____

3. _____

THIS PERSON BROUGHT ME JOY TODAY:

_____

I FEEL: ☺   ☺   ☺   ☹   ☹

WHAT WAS THE BEST PART ABOUT YOUR DAY?
DRAW OR WRITE ABOUT IT!

DATE: S   M   T   W   TH   F   S   ___ / ___ / ___

1. _____

2. _____

3. _____

THIS PERSON BROUGHT ME JOY TODAY:

_____

I FEEL: ☺   😐   😑   🙁   ☹

WHAT WAS THE BEST PART ABOUT YOUR DAY?
DRAW OR WRITE ABOUT IT!

Act of Gratitude

WRITE A THANK YOU NOTE TO SOMEONE!

DATE: S M T W TH F S ___ / ___ / ___

I'M THANKFUL FOR

1. _____

2. _____

3. _____

THIS PERSON BROUGHT ME JOY TODAY:

_____

I FEEL: 😊 🙂 😐 🙁 ☹️

WHAT WAS THE BEST PART ABOUT YOUR DAY?
DRAW OR WRITE ABOUT IT!

DATE: S   M   T   W   TH   F   S   ___/___/___

I'M THANKFUL FOR

1. _____

2. _____

3. _____

THIS PERSON BROUGHT ME JOY TODAY:

_____

I FEEL: ☺   ☺   😐   ☹   ☹

WHAT WAS THE BEST PART ABOUT YOUR DAY?
DRAW OR WRITE ABOUT IT!

DATE: S   M   T   W   TH   F   S   ___/___/___

I'M THANKFUL FOR

1. _____

2. _____

3. _____

THIS PERSON BROUGHT ME JOY TODAY:

_____

I FEEL: ☺ ☺ 😐 ☹ ☹

WHAT WAS THE BEST PART ABOUT YOUR DAY?
DRAW OR WRITE ABOUT IT!

DATE: S M T W TH F S ___/___/___

I'M THANKFUL FOR

1. _____

2. _____

3. _____

THIS PERSON BROUGHT ME JOY TODAY:

_____

I FEEL: ☺ ☺ 😐 🙁 ☹

WHAT WAS THE BEST PART ABOUT YOUR DAY?
DRAW OR WRITE ABOUT IT!

DATE: S   M   T   W   TH   F   S   ___ / ___ / ___

I'M THANKFUL FOR

1. _____

2. _____

3. _____

THIS PERSON BROUGHT ME JOY TODAY:

_____

I FEEL: ☺   🙂   😐   🙁   ☹

WHAT WAS THE BEST PART ABOUT YOUR DAY?
DRAW OR WRITE ABOUT IT!

DATE: S M T W TH F S ___ / ___ / ___

I'M THANKFUL FOR

1. _____

2. _____

3. _____

THIS PERSON BROUGHT ME JOY TODAY:

_____

I FEEL: 😊   🙂   😐   🙁   ☹️

WHAT WAS THE BEST PART ABOUT YOUR DAY?
DRAW OR WRITE ABOUT IT!

DATE: S M T W TH F S ___/___/___

I'M THANKFUL FOR

1. _____

2. _____

3. _____

THIS PERSON BROUGHT ME JOY TODAY:

_____

I FEEL: ☺ 🙂 😐 🙁 ☹

WHAT WAS THE BEST PART ABOUT YOUR DAY?
DRAW OR WRITE ABOUT IT!

DATE: S M T W TH F S ___ / ___ / ___

I'M THANKFUL FOR

1. _____

2. _____

3. _____

THIS PERSON BROUGHT ME JOY TODAY:

_____

I FEEL: ☺ ☺ 😐 🙁 ☹

WHAT WAS THE BEST PART ABOUT YOUR DAY?
DRAW OR WRITE ABOUT IT!

DATE: S M T W TH F S ___ / ___ / ___

I'M THANKFUL FOR

1. _____

2. _____

3. _____

THIS PERSON BROUGHT ME JOY TODAY:

_____

I FEEL: ☺ ☺ 😐 ☹ ☹

WHAT WAS THE BEST PART ABOUT YOUR DAY?
DRAW OR WRITE ABOUT IT!

Act of Gratitude

LIST 5 THINGS THAT ALWAYS MAKE YOU SMILE.

DATE: S   M   T   W   TH   F   S   ___ / ___ / ___

I'M THANKFUL FOR

1. _____

2. _____

3. _____

THIS PERSON BROUGHT ME JOY TODAY:

_____

I FEEL: ☺   🙂   😐   🙁   ☹

WHAT WAS THE BEST PART ABOUT YOUR DAY?
DRAW OR WRITE ABOUT IT!

DATE: S   M   T   W   TH   F   S   ___ / ___ / ___

I'M THANKFUL FOR

1. _____

2. _____

3. _____

THIS PERSON BROUGHT ME JOY TODAY:

_____

I FEEL: ☺ ☺ 😐 🙁 ☹

WHAT WAS THE BEST PART ABOUT YOUR DAY?
DRAW OR WRITE ABOUT IT!

DATE: S M T W TH F S ___ / ___ / ___

I'M THANKFUL FOR

1. _____

2. _____

3. _____

THIS PERSON BROUGHT ME JOY TODAY:

_____

I FEEL: 😊 🙂 😐 🙁 ☹️

WHAT WAS THE BEST PART ABOUT YOUR DAY?
DRAW OR WRITE ABOUT IT!

DATE: S M T W TH F S ___ / ___ / ___

I'M THANKFUL FOR

1. _____

2. _____

3. _____

THIS PERSON BROUGHT ME JOY TODAY:

_____

I FEEL: ☺ 🙂 😐 🙁 ☹

WHAT WAS THE BEST PART ABOUT YOUR DAY?
DRAW OR WRITE ABOUT IT!

DATE: S M T W TH F S ___ / ___ / ___

I'M THANKFUL FOR

1. _____

2. _____

3. _____

THIS PERSON BROUGHT ME JOY TODAY:

_____

I FEEL: ☺ 🙂 😐 🙁 ☹

WHAT WAS THE BEST PART ABOUT YOUR DAY?
DRAW OR WRITE ABOUT IT!

DATE: S M T W TH F S ___/___/___

I'M THANKFUL FOR

1. _____

2. _____

3. _____

THIS PERSON BROUGHT ME JOY TODAY:

_____

I FEEL: ☺ 🙂 😐 🙁 ☹

WHAT WAS THE BEST PART ABOUT YOUR DAY?
DRAW OR WRITE ABOUT IT!

DATE: S M T W TH F S ___ / ___ / ___

I'M THANKFUL FOR

1. _____

2. _____

3. _____

THIS PERSON BROUGHT ME JOY TODAY:

_____

I FEEL: ☺ ☺ ☺ ☹ ☹

WHAT WAS THE BEST PART ABOUT YOUR DAY?
DRAW OR WRITE ABOUT IT!

DATE: S   M   T   W   TH   F   S   ___ / ___ / ___

I'M THANKFUL FOR

1. _____

2. _____

3. _____

THIS PERSON BROUGHT ME JOY TODAY:

_____

I FEEL: ☺   🙂   😐   🙁   ☹

WHAT WAS THE BEST PART ABOUT YOUR DAY?
DRAW OR WRITE ABOUT IT!

DATE: S M T W TH F S ___ / ___ / ___

I'M THANKFUL FOR

1. _____

2. _____

3. _____

THIS PERSON BROUGHT ME JOY TODAY:

_____

I FEEL: ☺ 🙂 😐 🙁 ☹

WHAT WAS THE BEST PART ABOUT YOUR DAY?
DRAW OR WRITE ABOUT IT!

Act Of Gratitude

I'M THANKFUL I CAN...

DATE: S   M   T   W   TH   F   S   ___ / ___ / ___

I'M THANKFUL FOR

1. _____

2. _____

3. _____

THIS PERSON BROUGHT ME JOY TODAY:

_____

I FEEL: ☺   ☺   😐   ☹   ☹

WHAT WAS THE BEST PART ABOUT YOUR DAY?
DRAW OR WRITE ABOUT IT!

DATE: S   M   T   W   TH   F   S   ___ / ___ / ___

I'M THANKFUL FOR

1. _____

2. _____

3. _____

THIS PERSON BROUGHT ME JOY TODAY:

_____

I FEEL: ☺   🙂   😐   🙁   ☹

WHAT WAS THE BEST PART ABOUT YOUR DAY?
DRAW OR WRITE ABOUT IT!

DATE: S   M   T   W   TH   F   S   ___ / ___ / ___

I'M THANKFUL FOR

1. _____

2. _____

3. _____

THIS PERSON BROUGHT ME JOY TODAY:

_____

I FEEL: ☺   🙂   😐   🙁   ☹

WHAT WAS THE BEST PART ABOUT YOUR DAY?
DRAW OR WRITE ABOUT IT!

DATE: S M T W TH F S ___ / ___ / ___

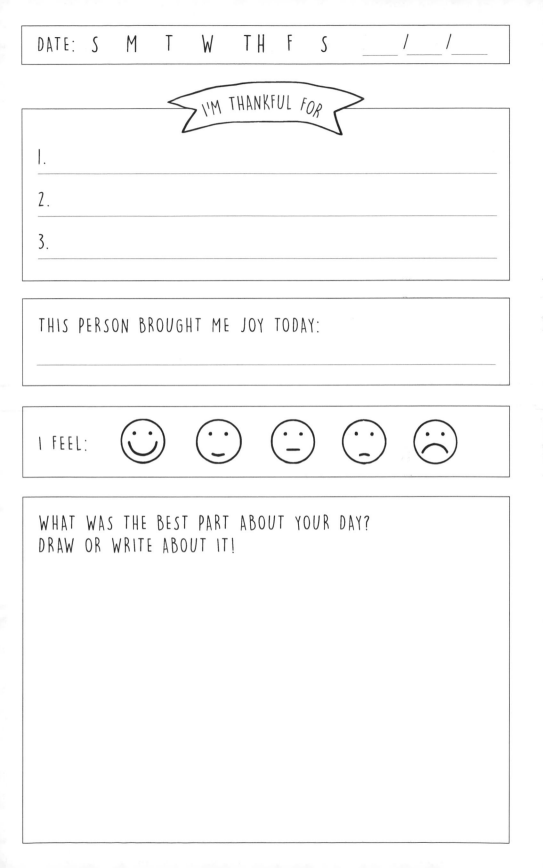

I'M THANKFUL FOR

1. _____

2. _____

3. _____

THIS PERSON BROUGHT ME JOY TODAY:

_____

I FEEL:

WHAT WAS THE BEST PART ABOUT YOUR DAY?
DRAW OR WRITE ABOUT IT!

DATE: S   M   T   W   TH   F   S   ___ / ___ / ___

I'M THANKFUL FOR

1. _____

2. _____

3. _____

THIS PERSON BROUGHT ME JOY TODAY:

_____

I FEEL: ☺ 🙂 😐 🙁 ☹

WHAT WAS THE BEST PART ABOUT YOUR DAY?
DRAW OR WRITE ABOUT IT!

DATE: S M T W TH F S ___ / ___ / ___

I'M THANKFUL FOR

1. _____

2. _____

3. _____

THIS PERSON BROUGHT ME JOY TODAY:

_____

I FEEL: ☺   🙂   😐   🙁   ☹

WHAT WAS THE BEST PART ABOUT YOUR DAY?
DRAW OR WRITE ABOUT IT!

DATE: S M T W TH F S ___ / ___ / ___

I'M THANKFUL FOR

1. _____

2. _____

3. _____

THIS PERSON BROUGHT ME JOY TODAY:

_____

I FEEL: ☺ ☺ 😐 🙁 ☹

WHAT WAS THE BEST PART ABOUT YOUR DAY?
DRAW OR WRITE ABOUT IT!

DATE: S   M   T   W   TH   F   S   ___ / ___ / ___

I'M THANKFUL FOR

1. _____

2. _____

3. _____

THIS PERSON BROUGHT ME JOY TODAY:

_____

I FEEL: ☺   ☺   😐   ☹   ☹

WHAT WAS THE BEST PART ABOUT YOUR DAY?
DRAW OR WRITE ABOUT IT!

DATE: S M T W TH F S ___ / ___ / ___

I'M THANKFUL FOR

1. _____

2. _____

3. _____

THIS PERSON BROUGHT ME JOY TODAY:

_____

I FEEL: ☺ 🙂 😐 🙁 ☹

WHAT WAS THE BEST PART ABOUT YOUR DAY?
DRAW OR WRITE ABOUT IT!

Act of Gratitude

MY NEIGHBORS

FAMILY   MY PETS

CUPCAKES   FRIENDS

MY TWO HANDS   SHOES

MY BICYCLE   SPAGHETTI

MY BROTHER

MY BED

ICE WATER

SUNSHINE   MY HOME

MY SISTER

DATE: S   M   T   W   TH   F   S   ___ / ___ / ___

I'M THANKFUL FOR

1. _____

2. _____

3. _____

THIS PERSON BROUGHT ME JOY TODAY:

_____

I FEEL: ☺   ☺   😐   ☹   ☹

WHAT WAS THE BEST PART ABOUT YOUR DAY?
DRAW OR WRITE ABOUT IT!

DATE: S M T W TH F S ___ / ___ / ___

I'M THANKFUL FOR

1. _____

2. _____

3. _____

THIS PERSON BROUGHT ME JOY TODAY:

_____

I FEEL: ☺ ☺ ☺ ☺ ☹

WHAT WAS THE BEST PART ABOUT YOUR DAY?
DRAW OR WRITE ABOUT IT!

DATE: S M T W TH F S ___ / ___ / ___

I'M THANKFUL FOR

1. _____

2. _____

3. _____

THIS PERSON BROUGHT ME JOY TODAY:

_____

I FEEL: ☺   ☺   ☺   ☺   ☹

WHAT WAS THE BEST PART ABOUT YOUR DAY?
DRAW OR WRITE ABOUT IT!

DATE: S M T W TH F S ___ / ___ / ___

I'M THANKFUL FOR

1. _____

2. _____

3. _____

THIS PERSON BROUGHT ME JOY TODAY:

_____

I FEEL: ☺ 😐 😐 ☹ ☹

WHAT WAS THE BEST PART ABOUT YOUR DAY?
DRAW OR WRITE ABOUT IT!

DATE: S   M   T   W   TH   F   S   ___ / ___ / ___

I'M THANKFUL FOR

1. _____

2. _____

3. _____

THIS PERSON BROUGHT ME JOY TODAY:

_____

I FEEL: ☺   🙂   😐   🙁   ☹

WHAT WAS THE BEST PART ABOUT YOUR DAY?
DRAW OR WRITE ABOUT IT!

DATE: S M T W TH F S ___ / ___ / ___

I'M THANKFUL FOR

1. _____

2. _____

3. _____

THIS PERSON BROUGHT ME JOY TODAY:

_____

I FEEL: ☺ ☺ ☺ ☹ ☹

WHAT WAS THE BEST PART ABOUT YOUR DAY?
DRAW OR WRITE ABOUT IT!

DATE: S M T W TH F S ___ / ___ / ___

I'M THANKFUL FOR

1. _____

2. _____

3. _____

THIS PERSON BROUGHT ME JOY TODAY:

_____

I FEEL: ☺ 🙂 😐 🙁 ☹

WHAT WAS THE BEST PART ABOUT YOUR DAY?
DRAW OR WRITE ABOUT IT!

DATE: S   M   T   W   TH   F   S   ___ / ___ / ___

I'M THANKFUL FOR

1. _____

2. _____

3. _____

THIS PERSON BROUGHT ME JOY TODAY:

_____

I FEEL: :)   :)   :| :(:(

WHAT WAS THE BEST PART ABOUT YOUR DAY?
DRAW OR WRITE ABOUT IT!

DATE: S   M   T   W   TH   F   S   ___ / ___ / ___

I'M THANKFUL FOR

1. _____

2. _____

3. _____

THIS PERSON BROUGHT ME JOY TODAY:

_____

I FEEL: 😊   🙂   😐   🙁   ☹️

WHAT WAS THE BEST PART ABOUT YOUR DAY?
DRAW OR WRITE ABOUT IT!

MIND YOU MANNERS AND BE SURE TO SAY THANK YOU TO
EVERYONE WHO HELPS YOU TODAY!

DATE: S   M   T   W   TH   F   S   ___ / ___ / ___

I'M THANKFUL FOR

1. _____

2. _____

3. _____

THIS PERSON BROUGHT ME JOY TODAY:

_____

I FEEL: ☺   🙂   😐   🙁   ☹

WHAT WAS THE BEST PART ABOUT YOUR DAY?
DRAW OR WRITE ABOUT IT!

DATE: S   M   T   W   TH   F   S   ___ / ___ / ___

I'M THANKFUL FOR

1. _____

2. _____

3. _____

THIS PERSON BROUGHT ME JOY TODAY:

_____

I FEEL: 🙂   🙂   😐   🙁   ☹️

WHAT WAS THE BEST PART ABOUT YOUR DAY?
DRAW OR WRITE ABOUT IT!

DATE: S   M   T   W   TH   F   S   ___ / ___ / ___

I'M THANKFUL FOR

1. _____

2. _____

3. _____

THIS PERSON BROUGHT ME JOY TODAY:

_____

I FEEL: ☺   🙂   😐   🙁   ☹

WHAT WAS THE BEST PART ABOUT YOUR DAY?
DRAW OR WRITE ABOUT IT!

DATE: S M T W TH F S ___ / ___ / ___

I'M THANKFUL FOR

1. _____

2. _____

3. _____

THIS PERSON BROUGHT ME JOY TODAY:

_____

I FEEL: 😊   🙂   😐   🙁   ☹️

WHAT WAS THE BEST PART ABOUT YOUR DAY?
DRAW OR WRITE ABOUT IT!

DATE: S   M   T   W   TH   F   S   ___ / ___ / ___

I'M THANKFUL FOR

1. _____

2. _____

3. _____

THIS PERSON BROUGHT ME JOY TODAY:

_____

I FEEL: 😊 🙂 😐 🙁 ☹️

WHAT WAS THE BEST PART ABOUT YOUR DAY?
DRAW OR WRITE ABOUT IT!

DATE: S M T W TH F S ___/___/___

I'M THANKFUL FOR

1. _____

2. _____

3. _____

THIS PERSON BROUGHT ME JOY TODAY:

_____

I FEEL: ☺ 🙂 😐 🙁 ☹

WHAT WAS THE BEST PART ABOUT YOUR DAY?
DRAW OR WRITE ABOUT IT!

DATE: S M T W TH F S ___ / ___ / ___

I'M THANKFUL FOR

1. _____

2. _____

3. _____

THIS PERSON BROUGHT ME JOY TODAY:

_____

I FEEL: ☺ 🙂 😐 🙁 ☹

WHAT WAS THE BEST PART ABOUT YOUR DAY?
DRAW OR WRITE ABOUT IT!

DATE: S M T W TH F S ___ / ___ / ___

I'M THANKFUL FOR

1. _____

2. _____

3. _____

THIS PERSON BROUGHT ME JOY TODAY:

_____

I FEEL: :)   :| :-   :(:(

WHAT WAS THE BEST PART ABOUT YOUR DAY?
DRAW OR WRITE ABOUT IT!

DATE: S M T W TH F S ___ / ___ / ___

I'M THANKFUL FOR

1. _____

2. _____

3. _____

THIS PERSON BROUGHT ME JOY TODAY:

_____

I FEEL: ☺ 🙂 😐 🙁 ☹

WHAT WAS THE BEST PART ABOUT YOUR DAY?
DRAW OR WRITE ABOUT IT!

Act of Gratitude

COMPLIMENT A FRIEND.

DATE: S M T W TH F S ___ / ___ / ___

I'M THANKFUL FOR

1. _____

2. _____

3. _____

THIS PERSON BROUGHT ME JOY TODAY:

_____

I FEEL: ☺ 🙂 😐 🙁 ☹

WHAT WAS THE BEST PART ABOUT YOUR DAY?
DRAW OR WRITE ABOUT IT!

DATE: S   M   T   W   TH   F   S   ___ / ___ / ___

I'M THANKFUL FOR

1. _____

2. _____

3. _____

THIS PERSON BROUGHT ME JOY TODAY:

_____

I FEEL: 🙂   🙂   😐   🙁   ☹️

WHAT WAS THE BEST PART ABOUT YOUR DAY?
DRAW OR WRITE ABOUT IT!

DATE: S M T W TH F S ___ / ___ / ___

I'M THANKFUL FOR

1. _____

2. _____

3. _____

THIS PERSON BROUGHT ME JOY TODAY:

_____

I FEEL: ☺ 🙂 😐 🙁 ☹

WHAT WAS THE BEST PART ABOUT YOUR DAY?
DRAW OR WRITE ABOUT IT!

DATE: S M T W TH F S ___ / ___ / ___

I'M THANKFUL FOR

1. _____

2. _____

3. _____

THIS PERSON BROUGHT ME JOY TODAY:

_____

I FEEL: ☺ 🙂 😐 🙁 ☹

WHAT WAS THE BEST PART ABOUT YOUR DAY?
DRAW OR WRITE ABOUT IT!

DATE: S M T W TH F S ___ / ___ / ___

I'M THANKFUL FOR

1. _____

2. _____

3. _____

THIS PERSON BROUGHT ME JOY TODAY:

_____

I FEEL: ☺ 🙂 😐 🙁 ☹

WHAT WAS THE BEST PART ABOUT YOUR DAY?
DRAW OR WRITE ABOUT IT!

DATE: S   M   T   W   TH   F   S   ___/___/___

I'M THANKFUL FOR

1. _____

2. _____

3. _____

THIS PERSON BROUGHT ME JOY TODAY:
_____

I FEEL: ☺   🙂   😐   🙁   ☹

WHAT WAS THE BEST PART ABOUT YOUR DAY?
DRAW OR WRITE ABOUT IT!

DATE: S M T W TH F S ___ / ___ / ___

I'M THANKFUL FOR

1. _____

2. _____

3. _____

THIS PERSON BROUGHT ME JOY TODAY:

_____

I FEEL: ☺ 🙂 😐 🙁 ☹

WHAT WAS THE BEST PART ABOUT YOUR DAY?
DRAW OR WRITE ABOUT IT!

DATE: S   M   T   W   TH   F   S   ___ / ___ / ___

I'M THANKFUL FOR

1. _____

2. _____

3. _____

THIS PERSON BROUGHT ME JOY TODAY:

_____

I FEEL: ☺   🙂   😐   🙁   ☹

WHAT WAS THE BEST PART ABOUT YOUR DAY?
DRAW OR WRITE ABOUT IT!

DATE: S M T W TH F S ___ / ___ / ___

I'M THANKFUL FOR

1. _____

2. _____

3. _____

THIS PERSON BROUGHT ME JOY TODAY:

_____

I FEEL: ☺ 🙂 😐 🙁 ☹

WHAT WAS THE BEST PART ABOUT YOUR DAY?
DRAW OR WRITE ABOUT IT!

Act of Gratitude

DRAW THE PEOPLE YOU ARE MOST THANKFUL FOR IN YOUR LIFE.

DATE: S M T W TH F S ___ / ___ / ___

I'M THANKFUL FOR

1. _____

2. _____

3. _____

THIS PERSON BROUGHT ME JOY TODAY:

_____

I FEEL: ☺ 🙂 😐 🙁 ☹

WHAT WAS THE BEST PART ABOUT YOUR DAY?
DRAW OR WRITE ABOUT IT!

DATE: S   M   T   W   TH   F   S   ___ / ___ / ___

I'M THANKFUL FOR

1. _____

2. _____

3. _____

THIS PERSON BROUGHT ME JOY TODAY:

_____

I FEEL: ☺   🙂   😐   🙁   ☹

WHAT WAS THE BEST PART ABOUT YOUR DAY?
DRAW OR WRITE ABOUT IT!

DATE: S M T W TH F S ___ / ___ / ___

I'M THANKFUL FOR

1. _____

2. _____

3. _____

THIS PERSON BROUGHT ME JOY TODAY:

_____

I FEEL: ☺ ☺ 😐 ☹ ☹

WHAT WAS THE BEST PART ABOUT YOUR DAY?
DRAW OR WRITE ABOUT IT!

DATE: S M T W TH F S ___ / ___ / ___

I'M THANKFUL FOR

1. _____

2. _____

3. _____

THIS PERSON BROUGHT ME JOY TODAY:

_____

I FEEL: ☺ ☺ 😐 ☹ ☹

WHAT WAS THE BEST PART ABOUT YOUR DAY?
DRAW OR WRITE ABOUT IT!

DATE: S M T W TH F S ___ / ___ / ___

I'M THANKFUL FOR

1. _____

2. _____

3. _____

THIS PERSON BROUGHT ME JOY TODAY:

_____

I FEEL: ☺ ☺ 😐 ☹ ☹

WHAT WAS THE BEST PART ABOUT YOUR DAY?
DRAW OR WRITE ABOUT IT!

DATE: S M T W TH F S ___ / ___ / ___

I'M THANKFUL FOR

1. _____

2. _____

3. _____

THIS PERSON BROUGHT ME JOY TODAY:

_____

I FEEL: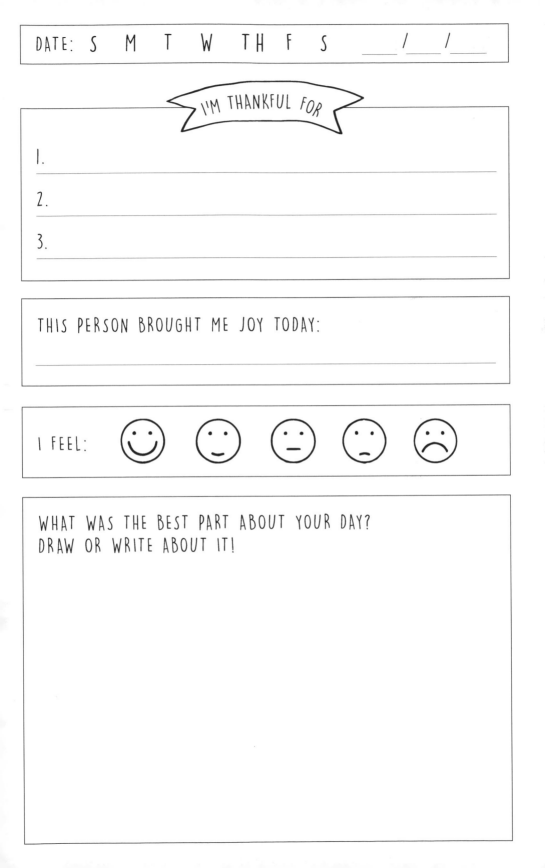

WHAT WAS THE BEST PART ABOUT YOUR DAY?
DRAW OR WRITE ABOUT IT!

DATE: S M T W TH F S ___ / ___ / ___

I'M THANKFUL FOR

1. _____

2. _____

3. _____

THIS PERSON BROUGHT ME JOY TODAY:

_____

I FEEL: 🙂 🙂 😐 🙁 ☹️

WHAT WAS THE BEST PART ABOUT YOUR DAY?
DRAW OR WRITE ABOUT IT!

DATE: S   M   T   W   TH   F   S   ___ / ___ / ___

I'M THANKFUL FOR

1. _____

2. _____

3. _____

THIS PERSON BROUGHT ME JOY TODAY:

_____

I FEEL: ☺   😐   😐   🙁   ☹

WHAT WAS THE BEST PART ABOUT YOUR DAY?
DRAW OR WRITE ABOUT IT!

DATE: S M T W TH F S ___ / ___ / ___

I'M THANKFUL FOR

1. _____

2. _____

3. _____

THIS PERSON BROUGHT ME JOY TODAY:

_____

I FEEL: 😊 🙂 😐 🙁 ☹️

WHAT WAS THE BEST PART ABOUT YOUR DAY?
DRAW OR WRITE ABOUT IT!

Act of Gratitude

TELL YOUR TEACHER WHY YOU'RE THANKFUL FOR THEM!

DATE: S M T W TH F S ___ / __ / __

I'M THANKFUL FOR

1. _____

2. _____

3. _____

THIS PERSON BROUGHT ME JOY TODAY:

_____

I FEEL: ☺ ☺ ☺ ☹ ☹

WHAT WAS THE BEST PART ABOUT YOUR DAY?
DRAW OR WRITE ABOUT IT!

DATE: S   M   T   W   TH   F   S   ___ / ___ / ___

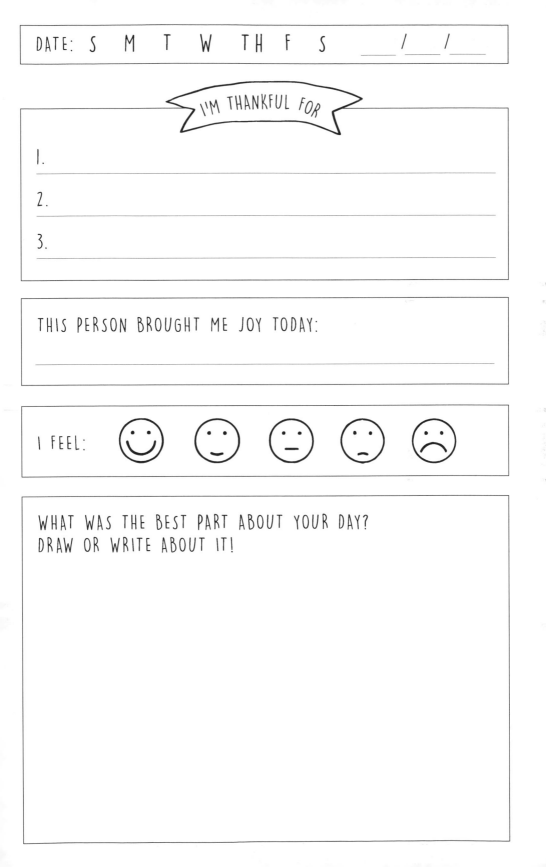

I'M THANKFUL FOR

1. _____

2. _____

3. _____

THIS PERSON BROUGHT ME JOY TODAY:

_____

I FEEL:

WHAT WAS THE BEST PART ABOUT YOUR DAY?
DRAW OR WRITE ABOUT IT!

DATE: S M T W TH F S ___ / ___ / ___

I'M THANKFUL FOR

1. _____

2. _____

3. _____

THIS PERSON BROUGHT ME JOY TODAY:

_____

I FEEL: ☺ 🙂 😐 🙁 ☹

WHAT WAS THE BEST PART ABOUT YOUR DAY?
DRAW OR WRITE ABOUT IT!

DATE: S M T W TH F S ___ / ___ / ___

I'M THANKFUL FOR

1. _____

2. _____

3. _____

THIS PERSON BROUGHT ME JOY TODAY:

_____

I FEEL: ☺ 🙂 😐 🙁 ☹

WHAT WAS THE BEST PART ABOUT YOUR DAY?
DRAW OR WRITE ABOUT IT!

DATE: S   M   T   W   TH   F   S   ___ / ___ / ___

I'M THANKFUL FOR

1. _____

2. _____

3. _____

THIS PERSON BROUGHT ME JOY TODAY:

_____

I FEEL: ☺   🙂   😐   🙁   ☹

WHAT WAS THE BEST PART ABOUT YOUR DAY?
DRAW OR WRITE ABOUT IT!

DATE: S M T W TH F S ___ / ___ / ___

I'M THANKFUL FOR

1. _____

2. _____

3. _____

THIS PERSON BROUGHT ME JOY TODAY:

_____

I FEEL: ☺ ☺ 😐 ☹ ☹

WHAT WAS THE BEST PART ABOUT YOUR DAY?
DRAW OR WRITE ABOUT IT!

DATE: S M T W TH F S ___ / ___ / ___

I'M THANKFUL FOR

1. _____

2. _____

3. _____

THIS PERSON BROUGHT ME JOY TODAY:

_____

I FEEL: ☺ 🙂 😐 🙁 ☹

WHAT WAS THE BEST PART ABOUT YOUR DAY?
DRAW OR WRITE ABOUT IT!

DATE: S M T W TH F S ___ / ___ / ___

I'M THANKFUL FOR

1. _____

2. _____

3. _____

THIS PERSON BROUGHT ME JOY TODAY:

_____

I FEEL: ☺ ☺ 😐 ☹ ☹

WHAT WAS THE BEST PART ABOUT YOUR DAY?
DRAW OR WRITE ABOUT IT!

DATE: S M T W TH F S ___ / ___ / ___

I'M THANKFUL FOR

1. _____

2. _____

3. _____

THIS PERSON BROUGHT ME JOY TODAY:

_____

I FEEL: ☺ 🙂 😐 🙁 ☹

WHAT WAS THE BEST PART ABOUT YOUR DAY?
DRAW OR WRITE ABOUT IT!

DATE: S   M   T   W   TH   F   S   ___ / ___ / ___

I'M THANKFUL FOR

1. _____

2. _____

3. _____

THIS PERSON BROUGHT ME JOY TODAY:

_____

I FEEL: ☺   🙂   😐   🙁   ☹

WHAT WAS THE BEST PART ABOUT YOUR DAY?
DRAW OR WRITE ABOUT IT!

DATE: S M T W TH F S ___ / ___ / ___

I'M THANKFUL FOR

1. _____

2. _____

3. _____

THIS PERSON BROUGHT ME JOY TODAY:

_____

I FEEL: ☺ ☺ ☺ ☹ ☹

WHAT WAS THE BEST PART ABOUT YOUR DAY?
DRAW OR WRITE ABOUT IT!

DATE: S M T W TH F S ___ / ___ / ___

I'M THANKFUL FOR

1. _____

2. _____

3. _____

THIS PERSON BROUGHT ME JOY TODAY:

_____

I FEEL: ☺ 🙂 😐 🙁 ☹

WHAT WAS THE BEST PART ABOUT YOUR DAY?
DRAW OR WRITE ABOUT IT!

DATE: S M T W TH F S ___ / ___ / ___

I'M THANKFUL FOR

1. _____
2. _____
3. _____

THIS PERSON BROUGHT ME JOY TODAY:
_____

I FEEL: 🙂 🙂 😐 🙁 ☹️

WHAT WAS THE BEST PART ABOUT YOUR DAY?
DRAW OR WRITE ABOUT IT!

DATE: S M T W TH F S ___ / ___ / ___

I'M THANKFUL FOR

1. _____
2. _____
3. _____

THIS PERSON BROUGHT ME JOY TODAY:

_____

I FEEL: ☺ 🙂 😐 🙁 ☹

WHAT WAS THE BEST PART ABOUT YOUR DAY?
DRAW OR WRITE ABOUT IT!

DATE: S   M   T   W   TH   F   S   ___ / ___ / ___

I'M THANKFUL FOR

1. _____

2. _____

3. _____

THIS PERSON BROUGHT ME JOY TODAY:

_____

I FEEL: ☺   🙂   😐   🙁   ☹

WHAT WAS THE BEST PART ABOUT YOUR DAY?
DRAW OR WRITE ABOUT IT!

DATE: S   M   T   W   TH   F   S   ___ / ___ / ___

I'M THANKFUL FOR

1. _____

2. _____

3. _____

THIS PERSON BROUGHT ME JOY TODAY:

_____

I FEEL: 🙂   🙂   😐   🙁   ☹️

WHAT WAS THE BEST PART ABOUT YOUR DAY?
DRAW OR WRITE ABOUT IT!

DATE: S M T W TH F S. ___ / ___ / ___

I'M THANKFUL FOR

1. _____

2. _____

3. _____

THIS PERSON BROUGHT ME JOY TODAY:

_____

I FEEL: ☺ 🙂 😐 🙁 ☹

WHAT WAS THE BEST PART ABOUT YOUR DAY?
DRAW OR WRITE ABOUT IT!

DATE: S   M   T   W   TH   F   S   ___ / ___ / ___

I'M THANKFUL FOR

1. _____

2. _____

3. _____

THIS PERSON BROUGHT ME JOY TODAY:

_____

I FEEL: ☺   ☺   😐   🙁   ☹

WHAT WAS THE BEST PART ABOUT YOUR DAY?
DRAW OR WRITE ABOUT IT!

Act of Gratitude

GO LAY IN THE GRASS AND ENJOY THE WARMTH OF THE SUNSHINE!

DATE: S M T W TH F S ___ / ___ / ___

I'M THANKFUL FOR

1. _____

2. _____

3. _____

THIS PERSON BROUGHT ME JOY TODAY:

_____

I FEEL: ☺ 🙂 😐 🙁 ☹

WHAT WAS THE BEST PART ABOUT YOUR DAY?
DRAW OR WRITE ABOUT IT!

DATE: S M T W TH F S ___ / __ / __

I'M THANKFUL FOR

1. _____

2. _____

3. _____

THIS PERSON BROUGHT ME JOY TODAY:

_____

I FEEL: 🙂 🙂 😐 🙁 ☹️

WHAT WAS THE BEST PART ABOUT YOUR DAY?
DRAW OR WRITE ABOUT IT!

DATE: S M T W TH F S ___ / ___ / ___

I'M THANKFUL FOR

1. _____

2. _____

3. _____

THIS PERSON BROUGHT ME JOY TODAY:

_____

I FEEL: ☺ 😐 😐 ☹ ☹

WHAT WAS THE BEST PART ABOUT YOUR DAY?
DRAW OR WRITE ABOUT IT!

DATE: S M T W TH F S ___/___/___

I'M THANKFUL FOR

1. _____

2. _____

3. _____

THIS PERSON BROUGHT ME JOY TODAY:

_____

I FEEL: ☺ 🙂 😐 🙁 ☹

WHAT WAS THE BEST PART ABOUT YOUR DAY?
DRAW OR WRITE ABOUT IT!

DATE: S   M   T   W   TH   F   S   ___ / ___ / ___

I'M THANKFUL FOR

1. _____

2. _____

3. _____

THIS PERSON BROUGHT ME JOY TODAY:

_____

I FEEL: ☺   🙂   😐   🙁   ☹

WHAT WAS THE BEST PART ABOUT YOUR DAY?
DRAW OR WRITE ABOUT IT!

DATE: S M T W TH F S ___ / ___ / ___

I'M THANKFUL FOR

1. _____

2. _____

3. _____

THIS PERSON BROUGHT ME JOY TODAY:

_____

I FEEL: ☺ 🙂 😐 🙁 ☹

WHAT WAS THE BEST PART ABOUT YOUR DAY?
DRAW OR WRITE ABOUT IT!

DATE: S M T W TH F S ___/___/___

I'M THANKFUL FOR

1. _____

2. _____

3. _____

THIS PERSON BROUGHT ME JOY TODAY:

_____

I FEEL: ☺ ☺ 😐 ☹ ☹

WHAT WAS THE BEST PART ABOUT YOUR DAY?
DRAW OR WRITE ABOUT IT!